YouTube Success For Teens

Start Your Channel, Become a Video Influencer, Have Fun!

Table of Contents

Introduction

Have you ever found yourself deep in the rabbit hole of cat videos, makeup tutorials, or epic gaming moments, thinking, *I could totally do this*? Well, you're right: you absolutely can.

I understand. You're always hit with the eternal question: What's up with life? But you have a dream of becoming the next YouTube sensation, and you know it's possible because of the thousands of other YouTubers. But deep down you are also asking yourself: *Can I really make it on YouTube? Where do I start?* Fear not: This book is the ultimate mentor that you absolutely need, the mentor that really gets you, your awkward moments, and the fact that sometimes you just want to binge-watch conspiracy-theory videos in your pajamas. YouTube is where dreams become memes and vlogging becomes a legit career choice! And we can conquer it.

Still skeptical? Well, let me drop some truth bombs. Even your favorite celebs started small, facing the same struggles you do. Imagine if Emma Chamberlain never dropped that first video or if PewDiePie thought gaming commentary was just a phase. This book isn't just a guide; it's your backstage pass to the world of those who dared to be different and made it big.

Imagine: you, with a gazillion subscribers, your own fan base, and a bank account that doesn't scream "college debt." This book is your shortcut to fame without the cringe-worthy trial-and-error moments. Imagine waking up to notifications blowing up your phone because your latest video just went viral. In this book you're gonna learn the secrets to creating killer content, mastering algorithms, and turning those crickets into cheers. Get ready to skip the line and jump straight into the spotlight—because who has time for obscurity?

Ready for the ride of your life? This book isn't just about views and likes; it's about unlocking your potential, embracing your quirks, and making a mark on the world. By the last page, you'll be full of knowledge, confidence, and strategy, ready to unleash your inner content creator.

Your journey to YouTube stardom begins now. Are you up for the challenge? If you've ever felt the burning desire to make your mark on the internet, then this is the right book for you. Let's turn those dreams into reality, one click at a time! Get ready to laugh, learn, and launch your YouTube career—fame waits for no one!

Chapter 1:

Getting Started

Since 2005, YouTube has evolved a lot while maintaining its core identity. Playlists were introduced in October 2005, quickly becoming a crucial tool for content creators. At the same time, the subscription function was integrated into the platform and this became the number-one motivating drive for creators. Despite adding and removing features over time, YouTube's popularity has soared, with T-Series holding the record for the most subscribers (211 million), followed, surprisingly, by "Cocomelon-Nursery Rhymes" (131 million).

Yet, thriving on YouTube doesn't always come with ease, even with massive subscriber counts. But you can find success by leveraging YouTube's features and using many different strategies. In this ever-changing landscape, you'll have to master the art of building influence on the platform. And this is where you will start by first creating your channel. Then you will set up some rock-steady strategies to keep going at a good pace. Lastly, you'll need to leverage YouTube's known and not-so-known features.

So, let's dive into it and start building a smashing YouTube page utilizing YouTube studio. But before you can create a channel, you should set rules that you will have to follow to be safe while using YouTube.

In most nations, YouTube is designed for individuals aged 13 and older. Those under 13 must wait until they meet the age requirement, yet they can still create videos. Although these videos can't be uploaded to YouTube, the advantage is that you can use this time for learning, experimenting, and practicing video creation.

For those aged 13–17 (varies by country), setting up a YouTube channel requires parental or guardian permission. Parents or guardians can assist by overseeing video uploads, comments, and channel interactions, ensuring a safe online environment. YouTube channels for kids have restricted features, such as disabled comments and community tabs, to prioritize safety.

It is recommended to keep YouTube video uploads private, with parents or guardians reviewing and approving content before publishing.

If you face any kind of cyberbullying or any form of bullying, including negative comments or content, you should talk to your parents, guardians, or teachers. If unsure about whom to approach, support groups for children provide a safe online space to discuss concerns (check the last chapter, "YouTube Support").

In case of discomfort from internet content, no matter how minor, you should inform your parent, family member, guardian, or teacher. Also, reaching out to dedicated support groups or contacting helpful online resources is emphasized. These support groups aim to provide a secure platform for children to express their feelings and receive assistance. Remember, these resources genuinely care about your safety and well-being.

Create a Personal Channel

When you decided that you wanted to start a YouTube channel, you had your own reasons in mind, right? But you should be aware of the fact that for any idea to prosper, you must have thought deeply through it, accounting for the possible challenges and the possible solutions, how are you going to sell it to your audience, and many more. This is a brainstorming stage.

Choose a Channel Theme and Name

So, before you create the channel, you need to spend some time thinking about your YouTube channel's theme and name. Being in the teen category, your channel theme and name will need to fit within the YouTube guidelines for 13–18-year-olds.

When choosing a theme, you should pick one that you truly enjoy. You should be genuinely passionate about it, as you'll be dedicating a lot of time contemplating, creating videos, and engaging with your community about it. Keep in mind that your subscribers are drawn to your channel because of their interest in that particular topic. If you ever try to change the theme along the way, be ready to lose some of your subscribers. That transition comes at a cost. You also don't need to choose a super-specific theme. This will limit you too much during your content creation. Your choice must be abroad enough to at least have different subtopics. You can use the following tips to choose the best theme:

- Choose a theme that you are good at or want to become good at.

- Choose a topic that other people are doing—and do it better.

- Choose a theme that no one else is doing.

- Choose a theme that solves a problem.

When you are picking a channel name, it is best practice not to use your real full name, which will help keep you safe online. However, you will also need to think of longevity, so while picking something that reflects your channel theme, choose one that will still be appropriate for you even when you're 40. Make sure that you don't rush this process. If you choose a name, and then decide to change it along the way, it will confuse your followers, and eventually you're likely to have some of them unsubscribe. Opt for a channel name under 20 characters for easy recall and typing. Ensure it's unique enough to stand out, steering clear of generic or overused options.

To be on the safe side, you must be careful and thoroughly think through this process. That is why you *must not* come up with all of this alone. You need people that have the best intentions for you and the most rounded sense of what will work long-term.

So, write down a few ideas that come to your mind, then go and discuss them with your family. They may also have some better ideas— you never know. They will actually become your first subscribers and number-one fans and will follow you even more closely if they invested in its inception.

Once you find your name, go and test it on your grandparents; this is a great test because if you're not comfortable saying it to your grandparents, then you need to keep looking. Use the following for brainstorming:

Practical

1. Some of the names I have thought of are:

    _____

    _____

    _____

    _____

    _____

2. My family thinks these are the safest names and have long-term potential:

    _____

    _____

    _____

    _____

    _____

3. Some of the theme ideas I have thought of are:

    _____

    _____

    _____

    _____

    _____

4. My family thinks these are the safest themes and have long-term potential:

_____

_____

_____

_____

_____

After getting your final ideas, you can choose the name that is best for you from those ideas.

Now that you've chosen a name and theme, let's guide you through the process of creating your YouTube channel. Follow these steps:

- Start by going to youtube.com or opening the YouTube app.

- Check the details, ensuring your Google Account name and photo are accurate, and confirm to create your channel.

With your channel created, let's enhance it and kick-start the content ideas inspiration process. Begin by uploading a main photo for your page. This image, whether a cartoon, an image, or a photo of yourself, will appear beside your name. Remember, it's your first impression, so make it a good one. Next, create a banner for your channel. This banner is what people see when they click on your channel; it serves as an extension of your channel's name and theme. This is a prime opportunity to sell your page and convert subscribers. Utilize free creative tools like Canva to design it. The banner should include your channel name and a short tagline explaining your theme. Adhere to YouTube's guidelines on sizing to ensure it displays correctly on different devices, especially mobile phones.

Before we proceed with the next step, let's navigate the platform and delve into its various features. Understanding these features is crucial for channel growth. Each plays a specific role in your success. Think of YouTube as your car, and just like you wouldn't drive a car without knowing its parts, you need to familiarize yourself with these features. They fall into two categories: YouTube Studios features, and YouTube

Browse features. So, grab a seat as we explore these YouTube features together.

YouTube Studio

Think of the YouTube Studio as YouTube's backstage, where the magic happens and your videos are organized with precision. YouTube Studio will help you fine-tune, enhance, and sprinkle a dash of optimization on your channel. It includes various features, described next.

Channel Dashboard

This is like YouTube Studio's command center. This dashboard is like the oracle of your digital world, tracking the performance of your videos and channel. It is where you go if you want to know what your most popular videos are. Also, this is where you go whenever you want to customize your channel and manage your videos—you can even send out a sneak peek of your next video to your community. By simply clicking the blue YouTube Studio button on your channel, you'll be led to the Channel Dashboard faster than you can say "subscribe." You can analyze which videos were a hit, which ones were a bust, and how well your channel is performing here. It serves as your digital crystal ball for insights into content strategy.

Channel Analytics

The Analytics tab in YouTube Studio is your data-driven compass. It won't magically conjure up views, but it will guide you in making informed decisions. You will be able to explore the depths of average view times, channel-specific views, subscribers, drop-off points, and demographic information about your audience. It's like having a digital Sherlock Holmes solving the mystery of viewer preferences. It will show you the numbers, graphs, and data. Did that explainer video top the charts while the product promotion flopped? Analytics will spill the tea.

Featured Video or Playlist Autoplay

Featured Video or Playlist Autoplay allows you to roll out the virtual velvet rope for new subscribers and returning fans. You can even customize a different video for newbies and loyal followers. It's like a VIP experience for your viewers. If you want to update this star-studded content, you have to hit the Customize Channel button on your profile. Besides creating a personalized journey for your audience, featured videos can score extra views if set to autoplay. Who said fame was elusive?

Online "Share" Button

The Online "Share" button is your cue to encourage viewers to spread the love on their social media platforms. With a simple click, viewers can share your videos and enable you to get more views and new subscribers. It's the built-in share function that turns your audience into digital promoters. After all, sharing is caring, especially in the YouTube universe.

Cards

These virtual calling cards will let you direct traffic back to your channel, other videos, or even external sites. Want to spice things up? Add interactive features like polls. It's like having a virtual Swiss Army knife for engaging your audience within the video itself.

Links in Video Descriptions

Just like linking your blogs to boost views, YouTube descriptions play the same role. You should drop those strategic links to your channel and related videos, with a quick description of each title. You can optimize your video and channel for search engines and improve the viewer's experience by hand-picking content recommendations for them. Include links to your channel or related videos along with a brief description for each title. This is a common approach used by popular YouTube personality Lilly Singh, host of "A Little Late with Lilly."

YouTube Browse Features

It is through the browse features that someone can reach and view your videos. So, to attract new audiences, it's crucial to rank on these features, enhancing views, subscriptions, and expanding your channel's reach. Let's delve into these features and discuss strategies for effective ranking.

Homepage

The homepage is personalized based on users' watch history and video-performance metrics. If you want to appear on the homepage, you should optimize your videos for YouTube search through strategic practices like natural keyword insertion in titles; tagging with popular keywords; categorization; custom thumbnails; and engaging elements like cards, transitions, and text. You should learn that utilizing highly specific tags will improve your channel's visibility—YouTube recommends videos in line with users' past interactions.

Subscription Feed

The subscription feed is where your new videos are showcased. In case you want to appear here, you should then go on and encourage viewers to subscribe through effective call-to-action (CTAs) overlays within videos, descriptions, and scripts. You must be consistent publishing videos to improve subscriber retention. Also, you should analyze video performance to understand audience preferences by checking the analytics and refining your content strategy over time.

Watch Later

This section is what keeps users engaged with your content similar to their current viewing. It relies on past viewing history and popular videos within similar audience segments. You have to optimize for Watch Later by using specific keywords and creating content with high views, subscriptions, comments, and likes. Building a strong YouTube community and engaging with your audience are very critical for visibility in this section.

Trending/Explore

The Explore page allows users to discover trending videos in categories like Music, Gaming, and Sports. Ranking here is challenging but achievable by increasing views and engagement. You should cross-promote videos through various channels, including blogs, newsletters, and other social media platforms. Hosting contests and collaborating with other brands can rapidly boost traction and expand your audience.

Other Browsing Features

Browse Channels is another section where users can find trending channels in specific categories. You have to properly label and tag your videos to rank in these features. However, engagement plays a significant role too; if viewers aren't interacting positively with your content, it may not be featured in browsing sections. So, be sure that you upload high-quality content to rank in these features.

Generally, to succeed on YouTube's browse features, you have to implement effective SEO strategies, encourage subscriptions, consistently produce high-quality content, and actively engage with your audience. Understanding the algorithms and user behaviors associated with each feature will enhance your ability to reach new audiences and expand your channel's influence.

YouTube SEO Optimization

As I mentioned in the previous section, you must optimize your videos and channels to enhance their rankings on YouTube's search engine. Search algorithms determine video visibility, impacting metrics like follower count, brand awareness, website visits, and revenue.

But what do we mean by SEO optimization? Optimization includes channel pages, playlists, metadata, descriptions, and videos. It goes beyond YouTube's search engine, affecting discoverability on Google, Bing, and others. Brands that have actually optimized for YouTube search trends have experienced a 50% growth in viewing time over the past three years (Brightedge, 2023).

To optimize for SEO, you have to leverage video text through transcripts, closed captions, and subtitles, which will emphasize relevant keywords. This will improve your vides' or channel's SERP ranks and audience engagement. Key tips include:

- optimizing video descriptions by finding the top two key words that describe your video and adding them into the title description.

- adding closed captions to each video by clicking the Subtitles button in your video details section. Actually, subtitles are always available for the viewer, but it is worth checking that they are correct, as many funny—and not-so-funny—errors have occurred.

- using Cards to promote related videos and engage viewers by adding interactive features such as polls.

- incorporating well-researched keywords naturally within titles, thumbnails, descriptions, transcripts, translations, tags, and links to increase the discoverability of the videos. Strategically placing keywords in calls will improve your video's relevance and search performance. This approach maximizes impact and audience engagement on your YouTube platform.

- selecting relevant video categories to reach target audiences effectively.

To enhance YouTube SEO success, you should consider factors like user engagement, CTA click-through rates, geographical viewership, and alignment of video and meta descriptions with user queries. YouTube search trends prioritize appealing videos based on total and current views, growth rate, source of views, and video age. Keyword research and implementation are very important for elevating video rankings on YouTube. You should embrace these tips to conquer the YouTube SEO landscape and propel your content to new heights.

Chapter 2:

Finding Your Voice

Now that you have your channel in place, let's work on your first video. You have probably heard of the phrase "Practice makes perfect" everywhere in this ever-changing content-development industry, right? Well, that is true. You should understand that excellence is a dynamic process rather than a fixed endpoint and that the journey to success is a bumpy one. That is why, when making your videos, you have to move through your fear and speak your truth—the audience will not only listen, but they'll love it. Trust me, this journey requires fearlessness, a rhythm uniquely your own, and the willingness to test, analyze, and grow through the process.

The first question you now need to ask yourself is, "What are my videos going to be about?" A piece of advice: You should always choose one theme and create videos about it. In saying that, you should be divergent around this theme—boring is as boring does. Essentially, what I'm saying is, if your channel is about funny cats, then don't put a live book read-aloud on it, because it's going to confuse your audience, and you will most likely lose followers. Likewise, if you want to make content that is more vlogger-style, uploading funny cat videos will make your community wonder if you're changing your channel's materials and hit that unsubscribe button.

Homework: Pick a theme and write it here to keep yourself on track. My theme is

_____

_____

Overcoming Fear

You now have a theme, WOO HOO! The next thing we are going to have to tackle is fear. Fear is the silent antagonist that often holds us back from expressing our true selves. Whether you're a budding content creator or a seasoned pro, the fear of judgment, rejection, or failure can be paralyzing. The first step on this transformative journey is to acknowledge that fear exists and is a natural part of the creative process.

Imagine fear as a shadow lurking in the corners of your mind. Instead of letting it consume you, bring it into the light. Understand that fear is not the enemy but a guide—a compass pointing toward the unexplored territories of your creativity. Embrace fear, for within it lies the potential for authenticity and connection.

To conquer fear, consider it a rite of passage. The audience doesn't seek perfection; they crave relatability. By sharing your fears, vulnerabilities, and imperfections, you create a bridge that connects you with your audience on a deeper level. It's the raw, unfiltered moments that resonate the most.

Creativity is the heartbeat of content creation, serving as the rhythm that sets you apart in the crowded digital space of millions of other creators. Just as a steady heartbeat signifies life, embracing creativity is akin to infusing life into your content. Moreover, it is through creativity that you can conquer fear, as it enables you to express yourself authentically and fearlessly. So, every time you feel afraid, redirect that energy toward the creation of your video. Instead of letting fear stop you, take one courageous step at a time, whether it's recording, editing, or pressing that upload button. Focus on the joy of the creative process, and with each action, you not only conquer fear but also move closer to sharing your unique voice with the world.

Embrace creativity as your ally in overcoming apprehensions, and let each creation be a testament to your authentic journey in the digital world. To unlock your creativity, embrace fearlessness—be unafraid to dance to the beat of your own drum. Utilize your creativity as a powerful tool to overcome apprehensions and reveal your authentic self to the world. Keep in mind, the world doesn't crave replicas; it yearns for authenticity, and your creative expression is the key to unlocking that genuine connection.

In this business of content creation, fearlessness is your superpower. It's the audacity to voice unpopular opinions, share unconventional ideas, and challenge the status quo. Remember, the most groundbreaking content often emerges from the willingness to embrace the discomfort of uncertainty.

Authenticity is composed of your unique perspective, experiences, and voice. Allow your content to reflect who you are, not who you *think* you should be. People connect with authenticity, and in a world saturated with content, authenticity becomes the magnetic force that attracts and retains an audience. Following are five straightforward tips to help you overcome the fear of creating content.

Recognize the Value of Your Content

The hesitation to create content often arises from concerns about aesthetics or the fear of not having enough to share. You need to recognize that your content inherently possesses value. Even if others may produce visually appealing videos, it doesn't diminish the worth of your unique perspective. Concentrate on sharing your content, and your authentic audience will find and appreciate it.

Homework: Jot down a few sentences outlining the key points you want to convey in your video. By writing them here, you'll have a reference when you hit the record button.

In my video, I want to emphasize:

_____

_____

_____

_____

_____

Embrace Simplicity in Video Creation

Just because a specific content format exists doesn't mean you must wholeheartedly adopt it. Whether it's traditional videos, shorts, tutorials, or live sessions, you should learn to choose formats that you have easy access to and can easily achieve while navigating through this fear phase.

Additionally, consider starting with one of the simplest types of YouTube videos: the talking head format. This involves speaking directly to the camera about a topic you're passionate about. It requires minimal equipment—just your camera or smartphone—and basic editing skills. This straightforward format allows you to focus on your message without the complexities of elaborate production, making it an excellent choice for those easing into content creation. Remember, the key is to choose a format that not only aligns with your comfort level but also allows you to share your unique perspective with your audience.

To enhance the quality of your talking head videos, consider keeping your head still while recording. This makes it easier to edit out any bits later on. Additionally, maintain a relatively close frame, creating a more intimate connection with your audience. This not only helps in establishing a personal touch, but also makes your message more engaging and relatable. Remember, simplicity can be a powerful tool in overcoming the initial hurdles of content creation.

Navigate the Unpredictable

Navigating the unpredictable terrain of a video's performance can be challenging. Instead of succumbing to overthinking, embrace the process of video creation. Over time, you'll realize that engagement is inherently unpredictable, and sometimes spontaneous content resonates more profoundly with your audience than meticulously planned videos. This realization marks a significant moment as you begin to relax more about your content creation, which leads to videos that feel natural rather than staged. It's a substantial step forward, and as you revel in this creative process, embracing its twists and turns, consider these tips to enhance your video's engagement.

Tips for Boosting Views in a Sluggish Video

- **Optimize thumbnails and titles.** Update your video's thumbnail and title to make it more eye-catching and intriguing. A compelling thumbnail and title can significantly impact click-through rates.

- **Leverage keywords.** Ensure your video is optimized with relevant keywords. This can improve its discoverability and help it surface in search results.

- **Promote on social media.** Share your video on various social media platforms to expand its reach. Engage with your audience and encourage them to share the video with their networks.

- **Create a playlist.** Group similar videos into a playlist. This can increase the chances of your video being recommended by YouTube, leading to more views.

- **Encourage subscriptions and notifications.** Remind viewers to subscribe to your channel and turn on notifications. This way, they won't miss any of your future content.

Remember, the journey of content creation is as important as the end result. Embrace the unpredictability, stay adaptable, and enjoy the creative process on YouTube.

Shift Focus From Virality to Consistent Sharing

Fear can take the format of the fear of not getting followers, so avoid fixating on the anticipation of a video going viral. Instead, you should adopt the mindset of sharing content without expectations of widespread recognition. What matters is consistently putting your content out there, allowing it to accumulate over time. The truth to content creation is maintained through your constant passion of what you are sharing, and as you become more experienced in sharing your story, your channel will grow.

Talk to a Specific Viewer in Mind

Rather than talking to a broad audience, envision a specific viewer who has reached out to you with a question or a challenge. Then, tailor your video content as a response to their inquiry, creating a personalized and relatable video and speaking specifically to them. Even if your video doesn't resonate with a large audience, it is more likely to significantly impact the type of individual out there searching on YouTube. This will help you curb your fear when recording, as it will help you focus on one individual.

Record, Test, Analyze, Grow: The Art of Skill Development

Okay, my friends, so now you have your theme, the words you want to say in your video and some tips to keep fear down. It's time now to make your first video. So, take a deep breath, face that camera, hit that record button, and share your unique voice by talking your idea out.

Congratulations on creating your first video! Now it's time to edit and feel satisfied with the outcome. Several free video-editing software options are popular for their user-friendly interfaces and versatile features. It's simply a matter of testing them out, finding the one that suits you, and experimenting with it. Remember, practice makes perfect, but it's not just any practice—it's intentional, fearless, and iterative practice. Keep in mind that the popularity of editing tools may change over time, and new ones may emerge.

Some widely used free video-editing software includes:

- **DaVinci Resolve:** DaVinci Resolve is a professional-grade video-editing software that offers a free version with powerful features. It's suitable for users of various skill levels, providing advanced color correction, audio post-production, and visual effects capabilities.

- **Shotcut:** Shotcut is an open-source, cross-platform video editor with a wide range of features. It supports a variety of video formats and has an intuitive interface. While it may have a steeper learning curve than some other free editors, it offers robust functionality.

- **HitFilm Express:** HitFilm Express combines video editing and visual effects compositing. It's a great option for those interested in adding special effects to their videos. The software is powerful but has a user-friendly interface, making it suitable for beginners.

- **Lightworks:** Lightworks is a professional-grade video-editing software that offers a free version with limitations. It has a simple and intuitive interface, making it accessible to beginners while still providing advanced features for more experienced users.

- **iMovie:** iMovie comes preinstalled on Apple devices and is a user-friendly option for basic video editing. It's especially popular among teenagers using Mac or iOS devices due to its simplicity and integration with Apple ecosystems.

Remember to check for updates and new software options, as the landscape of free video editing tools is continually evolving. Additionally, always ensure that any software you choose is compatible with your computer's operating system and meets your specific editing needs.

During this testing stage, you can refine your skills in editing, presenting, and storytelling. Testing is not merely a trial-and-error process; it's a strategic approach that will help improve your content creation. It involves experimentation, analysis, and continuous improvement.

Start by testing out your ideas during the editing process, no matter how unconventional they may seem. Break free from the shackles of perfectionism and embrace the messy, imperfect beauty of creation. Your first attempts may not be masterpieces, and that's okay. Remember, each video that you make is a stepping stone toward mastery. Editing is akin to storytelling; it's about crafting a narrative that engages your audience. Pay attention to the flow of your video, ensuring a logical, captivating sequence. Use cuts, transitions, and effects purposefully to enhance the storytelling experience. Consider the pacing: A well-timed edit can make a significant difference in maintaining viewer interest.

One top tip that I was given at the beginning of my journey was to add text during your videos. Not subtitles, but text that appears on your screen at certain points, providing more information about something you are doing or talking about. Doing this can visually break up the video and help keep your content engaging. For instance, you might display a quick tip or a fun fact related to your content. Or you could point out the product name of the cool thing you are using. To add a humorous touch, you might playfully highlight an incorrect word or slip-up by writing "Oops, I meant to say 'spectacular' here, but my brain had a little hiccup!" Furthermore, don't shy away from seeking feedback. Share your edited videos with others, gather constructive criticism, and learn from it. It's a valuable part of the iterative process that contributes to your growth as an editor. Embrace the journey, knowing that with each edit, you refine your storytelling skills and move closer to mastery.

It's now time to upload your video. Click CREATE "+" in the upper-right corner, and then select Upload videos. Choose the file you want to submit. A maximum of 15 movies can be uploaded at once. To change the details of your video, make sure you click Edit on each file.

The maximum resolution for your video will be used during conversion to guarantee smooth viewing across various networks and devices. The approximate processing times for SD, HD, and 4K videos are available for viewing. Processing times may increase for higher-quality inputs, like 4K or HD. Your movie will be preserved as private on your Content page if you exit the upload process before you've had a chance to select all of your preferences.

CONGRATULATIONS!! You now have your first video up on YouTube :).

Well, remember the analytics we talked about in YouTube Studio? It's check into the analytics of your video to examine audience engagement, watch time, and feedback. When you upload more videos over time, you will be able to see what worked and what didn't. Make that you don't use these insights as criticisms but as opportunities for growth. Your audience becomes a collaborator in your creative process, providing valuable feedback that shapes your future endeavors.

Always remember that skill development is the cornerstone of content creation. As you test and analyze, you refine your editing skills, honing the craft of transforming raw ideas into compelling narratives. Presentation skills, from voice modulation to on-screen charisma, evolve with each iteration. It's through this cyclical process of testing, analyzing, and growing that you cultivate the expertise required to captivate and retain your audience.

Audience Engagement

So, you've uploaded your first video. But how are you going to follow up its performance? Audience engagement, my friend! It's like a digital connection between you and your viewers. The more engaged they are, the more your channel shines. This engagement consists of the comments, likes, shares, and subscribers.

You've got to throw in some comments, respond to your subscribers, and, hey, maybe even spark a friendly debate that may become an idea for your next video. It's not always just about views; it's about building a YouTube community that vibes with your content. Ask questions, host polls, and create a space where everyone feels like they're part of something great. YouTube is like a hangout, where your audience becomes your digital BFFs. So you should not be afraid to dive into the comments and spark some conversations: you never know what may come out of it.

HOMEWORK: Write down how many people watched your video after one week and how many people engaged with (subscribed, liked, shared or commented) your video in that same time period. Work out the percentage of watcher to engagers. You are looking for around a 4% engagement rate—this will tell you that you are on the right track. Anything higher and get some feedback from friends and family about what to change or add for next time. Anything lower and you're golden, so keep going. Write your values here to give you a guide value to progress from.

_____ people watched my video.

_____ people engaged with the video.

My % engagement rate is _____.

Watch Time

Also, YouTube is not just about the number of views; it's about how long your viewers stick around to watch your videos. The YouTube algorithm has a soft spot for videos that keep viewers glued to the screen. Longer watch times signal to YouTube that your content is as addictive as Grandma's chocolate chip cookies. So, when you are making your video, keep it engaging, entertaining, and maybe throw in a plot twist or two. The longer people stay, the more YouTube will push your video into the limelight. It will be recommended to more people, which will actually increase the views and eventually subscribers.

HOMEWORK: Write down how many people watched your video after one week and the maximum number of hours your video was watched in that same time period. Work out the percentage of watcher to hours. You are looking for around a 50% watch time rate—this will tell you that you are on the right track. Anything higher and get some feedback from friend and family about what to change or add for next time. Anything lower and you're golden so keep going. Write your values here to give you a guide value to progress from.

_____ people watched my video.

_____ hours of watch time of the video.

My % watch time rate is _____.

Feedback

But hey, it's not all sunshine and rainbows. Feedback is like the spinach in the YouTube success smoothie—a bit hard to swallow but incredibly good for you. Whether it's thumbs-up or the dreaded thumbs-down, take it all in stride. You should understand that constructive criticism is your YouTube coach, and it will help you level up your content game. You should pay attention to the comments, learn from the feedback, and adjust your approach. YouTube loves creators who can take a hit, learn from it, and come back stronger.

HOMEWORK: Write down how many people watched your video after one week and how many how many people disliked your video in that same time period. Work out the percentage of watcher to dislikes. You are looking for less than 15% dislikes—this will tell you that you are on the right track. Anything higher and get some feedback from friends and family about what to change or add for next time. Anything lower and you're golden, so keep going. Write your values here to give you a guide value to progress from.

_____ people watched my video.

_____ people disliked the video.

My % dislike is _____.

Also, check through the comments, specifically the negative ones. Write down one negative comment, then analyze it to see if it is a constructive comment, or if it's just a troll. If you can see the light from this comment, let the person know you will work with their suggestion in your video. This is a great way to build a trusting community, and other people will respect you for it. I have converted annoyed people into loyal fans this way. The reverse of this is also useful.

PRACTICAL: A negative comment is

_____

_____

_____

In my next video, I will

_____

_____

_____

A positive comment is

_____

_____

_____

In my next video, I will

_____

_____

_____

Chapter 3:

Content Strategy

It's great that we have come this far and you already have your first video uploaded. However, I want to tell you that committing to YouTube isn't as simple as it sounds. You'll often find yourself in a state of total confusion or exhaustion, especially if you're hustling to stick to a crazy publishing schedule or aiming to level up your YouTube game. That's where a killer content strategy swoops in to save the day, giving you the freedom to innovate and grow your channel without losing your sanity. You can come up with this strategy after planning and considering your monthly schedule. You should understand that strategic planning is the linchpin of success that can help you achieve YouTube's triumph. It is a big factor in your content creation strategy. Creating a monthly content plan goes beyond mere post-scheduling; it is the cornerstone of effectiveness.

A content plan is a written strategy that contains details about the who, what, when, where, why, and how of your content marketing campaign. By having everything pre-scheduled, you will be able to gain the flexibility to invest more time in your channel growth. Remember, the main goal is to propel your YouTube endeavors to thrive. Here's a guide to creating impactful and goal-driven content for your YouTube success. The following are the seven steps you can go through to create a resourceful and impactful content strategy for your channel.

Set Your YouTube Channel Goals

To kick off your YouTube journey successfully, you must establish clear expectations for your channel. well, a key element of an effective content strategy is having specific goals rather than creating content aimlessly. These goals could be transitioning to full-time YouTubing, generating additional income through YouTube, consistently publishing high-quality videos, experimenting with new content types, increasing earnings beyond AdSense, or collaborating with fellow YouTubers. Depending on where you are on this journey, tailor your goals accordingly.

You should reflect on questions such as:

- What are my desires for my YouTube channel and its content?

- What does success mean to me in the context of my YouTube channel?

- How can I monetize this content beyond the confines of YouTube?

This introspection will give you clarity on your channel's purpose and how to attain it. Also, establish realistic and achievable goals with a defined timeline, ensuring a structured approach to your goals.

Homework: Grab a seat, then write your goals for this channel.

_____

_____

_____

_____

_____

_____

_____

_____

Get to Know Your Audience

Now that you have your goals in place, it is time to know more about your target audience. Do you want to generate content that is more in line with what your audience expects? Well, buddy! You have got to do some research. You may now be asking: what precise information about your target audience should you be looking for? Well, there are four key aspects you can look into:

- **Demographics:** This includes your audience's gender, age, and geographic location. When you understand these factors, you will be able to know the language and style best suited to reach them effectively.

- **Psychographics:** These include the traits that influence your audience's behavior, such as motivations, values, lifestyle, insecurities, and aspirations. Consulting reports, like those from Gartner, can be a valuable starting point.

- **Online behavior:** research about the kind of content and media that your audience consumes for entertainment, as well as the channels they subscribe to, the social media platforms they use, and the amount of time they spend on them. This information will show you how your target audience interacts with online information and guide your approach to engaging them.

- **Offline behavior:** You should look into your audience's buying behavior, habits, hobbies, current employment status, and preferred places to spend their time. This information provides insights into how to establish an emotional connection with your audience.

As you become more acquainted with your audience and their responses to your content, refine your target audience overview regularly. Evaluate your assumptions about your audience consistently.

You can leverage the audience you have on other platforms to obtain this information directly from them. For instance, you can poll your followers on LinkedIn, Twitter, and Facebook or using the Question Sticker on Instagram can be effective. If you follow some of those big YouTubers, you will see that they actually ask their followers about what thumbnail is the best, what title will sound catchier, or what the followers want the next video to be about. With this feedback, I assure you that you will be able to make a video that is directed to this audience. They will resonate most with your content. Over time, as you gain insights, refine your customer persona based on what you're learning from your audience.

Here is a challenge for you: I understand that you are on X (Twitter), Facebook, LinkedIn, or even Instagram. So, raise this question to your followers: What topic should I talk about in my next video?

_____

_____

_____

Spy on Competitors

Now that you've got the feedback from your followers and understand your target audience's preferences, what are your competitors up to? Time to check out other YouTube channels in your niche. This is going to inspire ideas for the content of the video you are to create. Go on and analyze what these channels are up to, and as you are taking notes. You can do this by:

- **Watching videos within your content niche:** Observe the types of videos, such as tutorials, long-form versus short-form, that creators in your niche are producing.

- **Subscribing to competitor channels:** Keep track of the frequency at which creators release new content.

- **Check the comments sections:** Read comments on competitor videos to understand how viewers are responding to existing content in your space. Identify areas where existing creators may be lacking, noting where you can excel.

- **Examining competitor video views:** Identify the types of videos that garner high views and engagement, essentially discovering the crowd-pleasers.

At the end, you have all the above down in your notebook. You can now start brainstorming diverse ideas for your video! You should generate many ideas to prepare for the next step. You should understand that YouTube is the optimal starting point, and the more time you are willing to invest in research, the better equipped you'll be for success. Also, note what works and what's missing in your videos.

In the long run, I recommend incorporating a variety of content types, such as how-to or tutorial videos, reaction videos, live streams, and opinion videos. This mix will not only keep your audience engaged but also position you as an expert in your niche.

Hey, it's challenge time: Sit down, brainstorm, and then write down 20 ideas for your next video in your notebook? Do it now before the next step.

_____

_____

_____

_____

_____

_____

_____

_____

_____

_____

_____

_____

Plan Your Content

Are you done with writing the ideas? So, let's now establish a content calendar, a schedule detailing what, when, and how frequently you'll be posting videos online. Choose 10 ideas from the previous step ("Spy on Competitors") and structure a publishing or uploading calendar around them. If your goal is consistent publishing, designate a specific day (e.g., Thursday) as your upload day—a savvy YouTube marketing tactic to build anticipation among your audience.

A well-thought-out plan not only aids in organizing your video content but also contributes to audience retention. By strategically linking videos through end-screens and playlists, you guide viewers to more of your content, keeping them engaged on your channel for longer periods. Flexibility is key, as industry updates or newfound ideas might prompt changes to your schedule. A nimble plan adapts to change, ensuring you stay on course.

You should incorporate a holistic approach into your content marketing strategy by assessing how each video aligns with your overall goals (remember those set in Step 1 "Set Your YouTube Channel Goals"?). You can use different monetization techniques for every video. You may develop a video especially for the affiliate program you participate in if, for instance, one of your objectives was to earn more money than just from YouTube advertisements. We constantly advise content creators to learn about the many revenue streams available to them. Because you'll need to look beyond video ads if you want to create content full-time. (Spoiler alert: ad revenue is declining, and demonetization is a major issue for creators.) Thus, be sure to consider other options that will enable you to monetize YouTube. This may consist of:

- affiliate links

- selling physical merchandise

- offering digital goods (such as access to your podcast or a subscription site)

- forming brand partnerships

Understanding these alternatives enhances your potential to generate income through YouTube, paving the way for a sustainable career as a content creator.

It's homework time: Based on your best 10 idea, design a plan on when you will record, edit, upload, and follow up the videos. Make sure to space out all these activities. Remember, it can't all be done in one day.

_____

_____

_____

_____

_____

_____

Bring Your Plan to Life

Now that your content plan is in place, it's time to bring those ideas to life! I've outlined a foolproof video production system in four simple steps:

1. Design Compelling Thumbnails and Titles

Once your ideas are laid out, you should now focus on creating enticing and catchy thumbnails and titles. Make sure that they are captivating enough to prompt clicks, as they are the first point of contact with your audience. These custom thumbnails play a crucial role in increasing your click-through rate, so you should consider making 2-3 options for each video. Your thumbnails should feature clear imagery, basic text with catchy keywords, vibrant colors that align with your brand, emotive faces, and an element of curiosity. Mixing graphics, keywords, and expressive faces can further enhance your video's impact. There's a lot of software choices that you can use, like Photoshop, Canva, Snappa, and many more. It is about choosing what is best for you.

Well, are ready for a challenge? I know you are. So, using a software of your choice, design thumbnails for these ideas.

_____

_____

_____

_____

_____

2. Your Video and Draft a Script

Next, you should then shift your focus to the actual video content. Whether you prefer outlining on paper or digitally, create a strong flow for your video, thinking about different frames and necessary props. After outlining, start drafting your script. Even if you opt for a more spontaneous style, having a script can make production smoother. Some videos may work better without a script, such as reaction videos.

Homework: Design a script for these ideas. Please take you time.

_____

_____

_____

_____

_____

_____

_____

3. Film, Edit, and Review

With your prep work complete, now it's time to shoot and edit your video. Bring everything together, clean up any mistakes, and make your video ready for YouTube. If you notice something missing or needing improvement during this process, don't hesitate to reshoot—it's part of the game. Investing time in editing is crucial for achieving high-quality videos. During this process, organize clips, add voice-over, remove unnecessary footage, incorporate intros/outros strategically, use cuts and transitions effectively, adjust color grading, and include on-screen text for viewer retention. Seeking feedback from advisors is valuable, as a fresh perspective can catch things you might have missed.

4. Hit Upload on YouTube

After completing the first three steps, it's time to share your video with the world! When uploading, be sure to turn on closed captions for accessibility. Keep a close eye on its performance in the first 24 hours to determine if any thumbnail adjustments are needed. In essence, these steps ensure your YouTube videos are not only well-crafted but also optimized for audience engagement and search visibility. The journey from planning to publishing is a creative process, and each step contributes to the success of your YouTube content.

Actually, before you upload the video, review the video and ensure that you have not left out anything. You must be contented and satisfied with it. You can take time off and watch it again the following day. By doing this, you want to ensure that everything you had planned for this videos has been done.

You should note that about 75% of the YouTube views come from videos recommended or suggested by the platform's algorithm. So, if you want to maximize your video exposure, make sure that you collaborate with the algorithm by creating compelling content paired with captivating thumbnails. The initial step in this process involves crafting attention-grabbing titles and thumbnails. For example, Mr. Beast who prioritizes creating thumbnails and titles that attract clicks. Even with a fantastic topic, if the presentation doesn't pique viewers' interest enough to click and watch, trust me on this, getting views will become a challenge.

Share the Love on Social Media

Wait! How are we going to let people know that you have uploaded a new video? Well, you remember your followers on social media who gave the idea to make the video? Yes, you have to inform them that you have actually uploaded the video. So, learn that whenever you post a new video on your YouTube channel, always consider repurposing it for your various social media platforms. Those followers are the ones you are making the content, and they have to know there is something new. This is an effective method for cross-promoting your YouTube content, and it will eventually end up attracting a larger audience to view your videos. This will lead to more connections within existing communities on other platforms. You should ensure that you are present on most of the social media platforms to create a bigger community. Here's a step-by-step guide on how to go about this:

1. **Choose your social Media platform.** Identify where your competitors are sharing content, such as LinkedIn or TikTok, and ensure your presence there as well. Starting with platforms like Facebook or Instagram is a safe bet.

2. **Conduct a competitor analysis on social media.** Once you've identified your competitors on social media, examine the content, the timing, and the interaction rates of your rivals. You may learn a lot from this analysis about the kinds of content that will probably be interesting to your audience.

3. **Identify repurposing opportunities.** Identify elements from your YouTube video that are valuable or shareable, exploring diverse presentation methods. This can include text-based posts, video snippets, and more.

4. **Include a call-to-action.** When sharing on social media, always include a call-to-action directing viewers to your YouTube channel. The ultimate goal is to generate excitement about your content, motivating people to watch the full video on YouTube.

The overarching objective is to promote your content with a genuine focus on providing value to your audience. Repurposing your videos for different platforms allows you to maximize exposure and engagement. This will ultimately driving viewers to explore your full content on YouTube.

Guess what it is? Challenge time! So, post on all your social media platforms, informing your followers about the new video.

_____

_____

_____

_____

_____

Check Your YouTube Analytics

You've done a great job informing your followers! Now, let's keep an eye on how well your videos are performing. Regularly checking your YouTube analytics is crucial for gaining insights into your channel's performance. It's recommended to do this at least twice a month. You're already familiar with the process from the previous chapter, but here's a quick checklist to refer to each time you check in during the month. This way, you won't miss any steps:

- **Overview:** Visit YouTube Analytics. Review the Overview section to get a snapshot of your channel's performance.

- **Traffic sources:** Check where your viewers are discovering your content (e.g., YouTube search, external websites, suggested videos).

- **Audience demographics:** Understand the demographics of your audience, including age, gender, and location.

- **Watch time and views:** Monitor your total watch time and views to gauge overall video performance.

- **Top videos:** Identify your top-performing videos and analyze what made them successful.

- **Subscribers:** Keep track of your subscriber count and analyze trends in subscription growth.

- **Likes and dislikes:** Check the engagement levels with your videos, including likes, dislikes, and comments.

- **Click-through rate (CTR):** Analyze your video's CTR to understand how effective your thumbnails and titles are in attracting clicks.

- **Revenue (if applicable):** If your channel is monetized, review your revenue performance and identify any patterns.

- **Set goals for improvement:** Based on your analysis, set specific goals for improvement in the upcoming weeks.

By regularly checking these analytics, you'll stay informed about your audience, understand what works best, and be well-equipped to enhance your content and channel over time. This would help you understand what adjustments are needed to steer your content strategy toward achieving your goals.

Chapter 4:

YouTube Algorithms

Are you still with me? Good. Now, let's try to understand what happens to videos backstage. Why is it that some videos are viewed more than others, yet they are uploaded at the same time or by the same person? This is the work of the YouTube algorithm.

First, you should understand that YouTube has the second-highest number of active users globally and has solidified its position as the premier video-first social media platform since its inception in 2005. Its ability to maintain viewer engagement shows how effective its algorithm is. Evidently, YouTube is employing a successful strategy with its algorithm. But what specific elements contribute to its effectiveness? What exactly is the YouTube algorithm?

The YouTube algorithm stands as an artificial intelligence–powered recommendation system that is designed to present the most compelling and top-quality content to its vast user base. This dynamic algorithm undergoes constant evolution, adapting to understand the unique preferences of each individual user. It relies on user preferences and engagement data, assimilating insights to determine what content a user wants to see more or less of.

So, understanding the mechanisms of this algorithm is key to optimizing your presence on YouTube. By aligning with the algorithm's principles, you can enhance the visibility of your content, ensuring it resonates with your target audience. You can not only successfully traverse the site but also take advantage of the algorithm's ability to elevate your work to new heights.

This algorithm aims to serve up the best and most relevant content to keep users hooked. But it also works in favor of the company's policies and values. According to the YouTube documentation, the algorithm has a heart, and it revolves around the four Rs:

1. **Remove** content that violates policies.

2. **Reduce** false news.

3. **Raise** up authoritative sources for news and information.

4. **Reward** trusted creators.

This means the YouTube algorithm is like your video bouncer, letting in the good videos that follow the rules, stick to the facts, and hail from trustworthy sources.

This algorithm is getting smarter, because it's built with machine learning, which helps the algorithm understand your viewer better than their grandma does. It's not about finding the videos for the users; it's about finding the users for the videos. When they stroll into YouTube, it's like the algorithm has their favorite pizza ready—ideas they're likely to munch on and enjoy.

But how does this magic happen? Well, there are two squads working behind the scenes: Viewer Personalization and Video Performance.

Viewer Personalization is like a video butler, noting down everything the users watch, ignore, and secretly love. It's like having a friend who knows your Netflix password—they just get you.

On the flip side, Video Performance is the cool kid who measures how much fun the users are having. It's all about satisfaction, baby! The algorithm is like a personal cheerleader, rooting for videos that make the users stay longer, share the love, and engage like it's a family BBQ.

So, how does YouTube gauge the user's satisfaction? Viewer satisfaction is determined by factors impacted by users. These factors might include metrics like these:

- longer watch time

- video shares

- engagement metrics (likes, comments, subscriptions)

- watch history

All these actions help boost the quality score of your videos and make them the stars of the show.

Now, let's investigate the inner workings of YouTube. It's not just a video dump; it's a space of personalized suggestions. So, we now know what the algorithm plays matchmaker, pairing the users with your videos. Let's break down each part of YouTube and discover how it works.

YouTube Search

It's an open secret that YouTube is more than just a video platform—it's a search engine in its own right. Beyond the search bar within the platform, YouTube videos are also prominently featured on Google Search Engine Results Pages (SERPs) and have a dedicated video tab for Google's video search. When you understand how YouTube's search algorithm works, it can be easy to introduce your video to audiences unfamiliar with your content.

YouTube emphasizes three key elements for effective search optimization:

- **Relevance:** Video title tags, descriptions, and search queries play a pivotal role. Think of these as your keywords—specificity matters.

- **Engagement signals:** Factors like video watch time help YouTube gauge a video's utility in addressing specific search intent. The longer viewers engage, the more favorably the algorithm views the content.

- **Quality:** Perhaps the most enigmatic element, quality is assessed based on signals that gauge channel expertise, authority, and trustworthiness. YouTube's guidelines underscore the importance of maintaining a high standard.

A captivating aspect of YouTube's algorithm is its consideration of individual preferences, evident in how search results vary between different devices.

Creators, such as Doug Dibert from Magnfi, share strategies for ranking videos on Google SERPs quickly. Dibert emphasizes the importance of utilizing long-tail keywords in various elements, including titles, descriptions, tags, and even the video file name. The video content itself plays a crucial role, with spoken keywords reinforcing the relevance to search queries.

YouTube Homepage

The YouTube homepage serves as the starting point for most users. For logged-in users, it offers a personalized experience with video ads, relevant content, and Shorts tailored to individual preferences. Unlogged users are presented with popular videos. Viewer personalization is key, with recommendations influenced by user data such as gender, age, and watch history.

Viewing a YouTube homepage with a signed-out user reveals prioritized videos based on how recently it was viewed, emphasizing the importance of staying current. Popular videos, evident in the screenshot, highlight the immense viewership they attract in a short span.

Recommended Videos

YouTube's Recommended Videos feature is a dynamic component that continually adapts. The algorithm considers various factors, including watch history, search history, channel subscriptions, and even geographic location and time of day. User engagement signals, such as clicks and video completion, are vital quality indicators for the algorithm.

Creators, like YouTube Strategist Zach Mitchem, stress the significance of the "Suggested Video" feature, responsible for 70% of views on the platform. Encouraging users to watch multiple videos from the same channel is a strategic move, signaling to YouTube that viewers are invested and prompting the algorithm to suggest more content from the channel.

Trending

Unlike personalized recommendations, trending showcases videos with a broad appeal. Achieving a spot on the trending list requires rapid video churn, often linked to viral content. Creators can leverage trending topics and "trend jacking" to increase visibility and capitalize on the current cultural or industry buzz.

YouTube creators, including Zach Mitchem, analyze the potency of trending videos and how strategic thumbnail templates can enhance a channel's success. Trend-focused content, coupled with visually appealing thumbnails, can significantly impact click-through rates.

YouTube Shorts

With the surge in short-form video popularity, YouTube encourages creators to embrace shorts. Utilizing YouTube-backed hashtags, like #shorts30, creators are prompted to upload daily, gaining prominence on the mobile homepage. However, the challenge lies in converting shorts viewers into long-form content consumers, requiring a delicate balance between short and extended formats.

Many successful creators highlight the potential of shorts but stress the difficulty in converting these viewers into long-form content consumers. Striking a balance between short- and long-form content seems imperative for broader audience reach.

Subscribers, Subscriptions, and Notifications

Increasing subscriber count and fostering an engaged following are paramount for creators. Subscribers receive notifications about new content, bringing them back to the channel and enhancing overall viewer retention. Creators can leverage subscription data to understand audience preferences, ensuring that their content resonates with the audience's interests.

Understanding that the YouTube algorithm finds videos for viewers, rather than the other way around, emphasizes the importance of analyzing which videos result in increased subscriptions. Replicating successful content strategies becomes a key component of sustainable growth on the platform.

Despite the importance of understanding algorithmic dynamics, there's a perilous edge to obsession. You, in a quest for visibility, might fall into the trap of constantly chasing algorithmic trends, sacrificing authenticity and creativity on the altar of views and likes. The danger lies in treating algorithms as an absolute, immutable force rather than a dynamic and evolving tool.

The fact is that algorithmic obsession can stifle your innovation and creativity, which reduces content creation to a formulaic exercise aimed solely at appeasing the algorithm. This approach, while initially yielding short-term gains, may lead to burnout and a decline in the quality of content. Viewers can sense when content is produced merely to cater to algorithmic preferences, eroding the trust between creators and their audience.

In this journey, just make sure that you do not obsess over this YouTube algorithm. Innovation and quality are key.

Chapter 5:

Is Consistency Key?

If you've done some research about how to grow a YouTube channel, chances are a lot of people have emphasized the significance of consistency on this platform. Is there truly a payoff for maintaining a consistent uploading schedule on YouTube? Absolutely. That's why the emphasis on consistency is so huge. But just how pivotal is it, and is the exertion invested justified by the rewards?

If you want to become successful on YouTube, you'll need to regularly release new videos. You should understand that consistency will always stand out as a cornerstone in your channel growth, and YouTube duly acknowledges and rewards it. Therefore, if you have aspirations of success, prioritizing consistency becomes paramount to increasing your views, subscribers, and overall channel expansion.

However, the importance of consistency goes beyond mere audience appreciation for regular content. Contrary to popular belief, its impact is deeply rooted in technical aspects that extend beyond the apparent satisfaction of your viewers with a steady stream of new content. While audience engagement is undoubtedly a positive outcome, consistent uploads will yield benefits that go beyond the surface level, which will contribute to the technical complexities that underpin a successful YouTube channel.

What makes consistency important on YouTube? Is it merely due to viewers favoring regular uploads from their subscribed channels? Or does its significance extend beyond viewer preferences into more technical aspects? While it is true that viewers appreciate a consistent upload schedule from channels they subscribe to, the importance of consistency on YouTube has a deeper, more technical underpinning.

As highlighted in the previous chapter, the YouTube algorithm plays a big role in determining a channel's growth. Consequently, as a content creator, it is imperative to align efforts with the goal of satisfying the YouTube algorithm. Consistent uploading, when coupled with adherence to other best practices, serves to meet the algorithm's criteria.

The YouTube algorithm evaluates various metrics to gauge the quality of a video. These metrics encompass factors such as views, watch time, average view duration, click-through rate, and more. Accumulating satisfactory metrics is a gradual process, but the consistent publication of videos expedites the timeline for building up these crucial indicators.

Often, most creators generate a YouTube channel with the intention of rapidly growing their audience. However, many are unprepared for the protracted journey that every content creator must undertake to achieve success. Consistency is not a practice confined to short-term gains; rather, it is an essential commitment if you are aiming for sustained success in the long run.

If rapid audience growth is your goal, then you should recognize that success on YouTube is a marathon rather than a sprint. Establishing consistency over the long term becomes paramount for those who seek enduring success.

It's no secret that maintaining a regular YouTube posting schedule may be challenging. There is a lot of work to be done, including making videos, designing thumbnails, and optimizing your videos!

Basing on my experience, ever since I started using YouTube, I've picked up a few tips regarding how to regularly upload videos. The following tips have made it considerably easier for me and many other content providers to regularly submit fresh videos to the internet. So, try these suggestions and see if they can assist you!

Organization Is Key

You may find yourself in a dilemma of not knowing what to create a video about when you turn on your camera or microphone. Just know that you're not alone. Many content creators struggle with consistent video uploads due to a lack of organization. The key solution to this challenge lies in becoming more organized. By taking the time to compile a list of topics in advance, you can avoid the uncertainty of not knowing what to create videos about. To enhance your consistency in uploading videos, ensure you always have a readily available list of video topics, preventing the common issue of starting a recording without a clear direction.

Batch, Batch, Batch

Just imagine recording a video at 4:00 p.m., editing it, optimizing it, and then uploading it at 7:00 p.m. This leads to eventual burnout and lowers the quality of your videos. You will start struggling with efficiency at this point. A solution to this challenge lies in the practice of batching. Successful YouTube creators leverage batching by dedicating specific periods to one task before moving on to the next. For instance, recording videos for an entire week before initiating the editing process. Many accomplished creators go further, batching enough videos to sustain them for a month. You should understand that batching extends beyond recording; it's equally beneficial for editing and optimizing videos.

Create a Schedule

When addressing YouTube schedules, we often focus on publishing or upload schedules. However, considering other aspects of YouTube, establishing a video creation schedule can significantly streamline the process. Many successful channels adopt a structured approach by recording all their videos on one day, editing on another, optimizing on a specific day, and, finally, handling thumbnail design, end screens, and cards. This rotational process is often repeated, commonly in video creation batches.

It's worth noting that, while some creators dedicate entire days to specific tasks, this might not be feasible for everyone, especially if you have other commitments like a job or school. In such cases, creating an hourly schedule could be a more realistic approach. For instance, allocating every weekday from 5:30 to 6:30 p.m. for YouTube tasks can be an effective way to manage your time.

Homework: For the next month, you must be consistent with posting videos. Do you remember the 10 ideas that you shortlisted? It is time to release four of them this month. So, following the above tips, ensure that they are uploaded on time as per your schedule.

It would be beneficial for you to release videos as frequently as you can. Does consistency get rewarded on YouTube? Indeed, it does. Thus, it's best to start receiving consistent views as soon as possible. But you may find this to be a challenging task. So, make an effort to organize yourself better, experiment with batching, and make a YouTube timetable for yourself.

Chapter 6:

How to Make a Perfect Video

For a video to be successful, it must have good and clear quality as well as good audio. When you look through most of the videos on YouTube, you realize that most of the big names have heavily invested in their production. And these are the people you are going to compete with. But fear not—you can actually make good-quality videos and even outcompete them with just a few pieces of (relatively) inexpensive equipment: an iPhone, tripod, simple microphone, lighting, a white piece of paper, and editing software.

iPhone: You can start by using your iPhone camera. An iPhone can make better-quality videos compared to some of the low-budget cameras.

Tripod: Stabilizing your camera is imperative for improved footage, which is why you should consider a tripod. A tripod is ideal for stationary setups.

Microphone: While commencing with phone recording is acceptable, you should get a quality microphone to enhance video quality with clear audio and expanded editing possibilities. For dialogue-focused content, a lavalier microphone is the best option, and for handheld work, a shotgun mic is the best option.

Lighting: To achieve a polished visual aesthetic, you can use two softboxes on either side of the camera. Alternatively, budget-friendly ring lights can impart a gentle glow to a single subject. For enhanced lighting control, an investment in an LED kit with dimming and color warmth options is advocated.

Utilizing a white card at the beginning for color correction: Incorporate a white card into your filming setup at the start of your video. Simply hold it up for a couple of seconds and then place it back down. This simple action provides a valuable reference point for color correction and white balance adjustments during post-production. By adopting this technique, you guarantee that your video not only looks visually pleasing after editing but also streamlines the color correction process for a more polished final result.

Editing software: When it comes to editing tools, Adobe Premiere Pro is a good choice because of its advanced features and user-friendly interface, making it appropriate for both pros and beginners. iMovie is a great place for beginners to start if they're looking for a free resource to learn the fundamentals before committing to a commercial program.

Filming Tips

To make the best videos, we offer a few tips for you to take into consideration. These items are as important to your success as the equipment.

Use Enough Light

You should make sure that you make effective lighting a priority; it greatly improves the quality of your video. Keep in mind that inadequate or poorly positioned light can diminish the overall professionalism of your video, even if other factors are excellent.

When you are working with natural light, the sun serves as an excellent source—the best times to film a video are in the morning or evening, as the softer light during these periods avoids harsh shadows cast by midday sunlight directly overhead. If you want to film during midday, you should consider cloudy conditions or finding shaded areas for a gentler light.

For indoor filming, consider different lighting types and placements. Make sure that you avoid overhead lighting, as it can create unflattering shadows. Use windows for natural light or incorporate large lamps or ring lights strategically around yourself to achieve the desired lighting effect.

Before setting up your lighting, contemplate the desired impact on your video's final appearance. Decide whether you want even illumination ("soft" or "flat" light) or if you prefer some shadows ("hard" light).

Usually, in professional videos, excessive shadow usage can create a dramatic but potentially distracting effect. For business and marketing videos, a more open and straightforward vibe is often preferable, which can be achieved by minimizing or eliminating shadows.

For flat light, you should position two light sources on either side of the camera, creating a balanced effect with minimal shadows. Alternatively, if you seek more shadow and depth, employ the "lighting triangle" technique to achieve the desired visual impact.

Use a Clean Background

When you are choosing your filming background, make sure that you maintain a professional appearance. A cluttered or distracting background will detract from your video's quality. That's why you should opt for a solid-colored backdrop, utilizing a wall, a bedsheet, or backdrop paper (preferably white) for a polished look. Position yourself several feet away to prevent shadows on the back. Also, avoid filming with windows or reflective surfaces in the background to prevent unintended reflections, and refrain from placing a light source, like having a window behind you, as it can result in a dark and shadowy appearance.

Choose Good Video-Editing Software

You should select good video-editing software to transform your raw footage into a polished final product. Consider the unpaid versions of software for simpler editing needs. When choosing a video editor, focus on key features such as text addition, video trimming and cropping capabilities, scene transitions, aspect ratio adjustment, and the availability of filters, overlays, as well as a library of stock videos and sounds.

Keep Your Editing Simple

While editing a video, experimenting with various effects can be fun, but don't get carried away. You should learn that professional editing usually has a clean and basic aesthetic. You just need to do a few edits at this stage:

- Any background noise can be eliminated by using noise cancellation.

- If necessary, adjust the lighting a little.

- Eliminate uncomfortable silences and pauses.

- Transitions and background music should be added.

Ensure to make the cut whenever there is motion in both areas of your professional video. Compared to hopping from one scene where nothing is happening to another, this is more fluid and organic.

Prioritize Crisp, Clear Audio

In all honesty, audio quality is more important than video quality. Many people can stay and continue watching a poor-quality video as long as everything else about it is good. But no one can tolerate a video with poor audio, which is why you need to buy a microphone.

Place your microphone as close to your mouth as you can to get quality audio. For the final recording, you may wish to use a pop filter to remove blips and crackles. Additionally, be mindful of any background sounds that your microphone may be taking up.

Even while it's simple to ignore sounds like birds, traffic, and wind, your recording will clearly emit all of these sounds. So, you should be careful with your environment.

Avoid Shaky Footage

Shaky footage will make your video appear amateurish, which might even give your viewers motion sickness. It's difficult to hold a camera perfectly steady; therefore, if at all possible, try not to hold your camera. Alternatively, place your camera on a stable surface or use a tripod.

Try not to move your camera once it is set up unless absolutely necessary. Constant panning takes away from a video's polished appearance. If you need to switch perspectives, it's preferable to cut from one scene to another rather than moving the camera.

If, despite your best efforts, your footage still comes out shaky, video-stabilization software can help you fix it later. Slowing down your video might also help to hide shakiness.

Use Your Phone the Right Way

You don't have DSLR camera? Not an issue. Good-quality video footage may be recorded with your phone; it works well for most uses. However, there are a few considerations to make if you plan to create videos with your phone:

- Make use of your phone's back camera.

- Take notes in landscape mode, which is to say, horizontally rather than vertically. This will provide you with video that looks great on displays larger than those on phones.

- Use the capability on your phone to overlay a grid on your screen, if it exists. By doing this, you can prevent skewed video and maintain your phone level.

Work on Your Camera Presence

The way you conduct yourself on camera has a big influence on how engaging your videos will appear. Making uneasy, fidgety, or uncomfortable faces while speaking on television will draw attention away from your message.

You absolutely can get better at this with experience. If your camera presence is lacking, here are some key points to consider when filming:

- Use serene, honest body language. Keep your posture upright; a bad camera angle will quickly become apparent. Maintain your muscles relaxed and your shoulders back. Inhale deeply. Avoid crossing your arms—this gives off a closed-off vibe.

- Smile, particularly at the start of your video. It has a significant impact on your perceived friendliness.

- When speaking, try to pronounce well and speak a little more slowly. Instead of speaking from your throat, use your diaphragm.

- Try utilizing props to occupy your hands, if you're nervous. For example, writing on a whiteboard can help you divert your attention from the camera.

Take Videos From Different Angles

A nice and easy method to give your videos more visual interest is to cut between different angles. If you're creating a how-to video, a product demo, or any other kind of video where you're doing something instead of just talking, this is a very helpful strategy.

Make sure to capture an ample amount of B-roll for every film you produce, so you can utilize it later, if desired.

Be sure to rotate your angle at least 45 degrees when you do so. These smaller perspective changes merely give the impression of being startling to the viewers rather of having the desired effect.

Although creating good-quality videos requires some experience and knowledge, it is not magic or rocket science; it won't take you years to learn. You can improve the quality of your next video by employing the simple procedures described above.

Homework: Write down what equipment you have.

_____

_____

_____

_____

_____

_____

Following all that we have discussed, make a video and compare it with your previous videos. Then answer this question: Is the video better than the previous videos? (Yes or No)

Chapter 7:

Talk to Your Viewers

So, you've got your YouTube channel up and running, pumping out content that you're pretty proud of. But here's the thing—your viewership feels a bit like a one-way street. You're sending videos out into the vastness of the internet, but it seems like you're missing the memo on building a community. Well, if you're not talking to your viewers through comments, you're missing out on a golden ticket to grow your audience and create a squad of loyal fans.

Think about it. When we hear the word "schedules" in the YouTube world, our minds jump straight to publishing schedules—when to drop that new video, right? But what about scheduling some quality time with your audience? Yup, it's time to start a conversation. Creating a video creation schedule is cool and all, but carving out space to chat with your viewers is like the secret to building a fanbase that's more loyal than your grandma's dog.

Now, let's take a peek into the big-shot YouTubers—you know, the ones with millions of subscribers who seem to have it all figured out. Guess what? They've cracked the code, and it's all about turning your channel into a digital hangout spot. So, how do they do it? Well, they're not just posting videos and ghosting. No sir, they're talking to their viewers like it's a never-ending virtual party.

As mentioned in the previous chapter, many of those YouTube giants have a routine. They pick a day to shoot all their videos, another day to edit like mad scientists, a specific day to sprinkle some optimization magic, and finally, a day to pimp out their videos with snazzy thumbnails, end screens, and cards. It's like a video production assembly line, and it works like a charm.

But here's the juicy part—they're not just hitting "Upload" and calling it a day. Nope, they dive into the comments section. They're responding to comments, hearting the good vibes, and sometimes even throwing in a sassy comeback or two. It's like they've set up camp in the comments, and everyone's invited to the party.

Why bother, you ask? Well, this is where the magic happens. Engaging with your audience through comments isn't just about being polite (although manners are always in style). It's about creating a connection, forging a bond, and turning those one-time viewers into a crew that's ride-or-die for your content. It's about building a community around your channel.

Think about it from a viewer's perspective: You're scrolling through YouTube, stumble upon a cool video, and decide to drop a comment. Lo and behold, the creator not only notices your comment but responds with something witty or a heartfelt thank you. Suddenly, you're not just a random viewer; you're part of the conversation. You're acknowledged, appreciated, and that creator just earned some serious brownie points in your book.

But, hey, I get it. You might be thinking, "I've got a job, a life, and a pet rock to take care of. How can I possibly spend all day in the comments section?" Fair point. The big creators might have the luxury of dedicating entire days to their YouTube empire, but for us mere mortals, an hourly schedule could be the game-changer.

Imagine this: every weekday from 5:30 PM to 6:30 PM becomes your sacred YouTube time. You're not just mindlessly scrolling through cat videos (although, let's be real, those are irresistible). Nope, you're engaging with your viewers, replying to comments, and making your corner of the internet a welcoming space.

It's not just about responding to comments; it's about sparking conversations. Throw out some questions in your videos—get your audience talking. What's their favorite part of your latest upload? Any wild theories about your next project? It's like giving them a backstage pass to your creative process.

Now, here's a nugget of wisdom: consistency isn't just for posting videos. It applies to engaging with your audience too. Make it a routine, a habit. Your viewers will start expecting your digital chatting sessions, and trust us, they'll keep coming back for more.

Leaving comments on YouTube videos is more than just a digital thumbprint; it's a strategic move that can elevate your online presence in numerous ways. Here's the lowdown on the benefits of joining the conversation on other people's videos:

You establish yourself as an expert.

First and foremost, it's your ticket to establishing yourself as an expert in your field. When you craft comments that are not just well-written but also smart and brimming with useful information, you're essentially showcasing your knowledge to the world. Think about it as your mini–TED talk in the comment section. Others notice when you bring valuable insights to the table, and if you consistently do so, you might find yourself becoming the go-to person for advice. It's like having your own corner of the internet where people seek your expertise.

You connect with new people.

Beyond showcasing your expertise, leaving comments is a direct pipeline to connecting with new people. It's a free, fast, and accessible way to make your voice heard by an entirely fresh audience. Whether you're dropping wisdom, cracking jokes, or just offering a different perspective, your comments can serve as a virtual icebreaker. You're not just a silent viewer anymore; you're an active participant in the digital dialogue, and that can be a game-changer in expanding your social circle.

You will increase your video views and profile views.

Now, let's talk numbers—specifically, your video and profile views. Engaging comments that stand out can act as a magnet for curious viewers. If you say something interesting, unique, or downright intriguing, fellow readers might click on your profile to see what else you're about. And what do they find? Your videos. Your channel. Before you know it, your video views and profile views are climbing, and if your content resonates, you might gain some new subscribers. It's like a domino effect triggered by a well-crafted comment.

You will see what's popular on YouTube.

But it's not just about self-promotion; it's about being part of the YouTube ecosystem. Commenting on others' videos within your industry or niche exposes you to what's hot and happening on the platform. It's a window into the trends, discussions, and innovations that are shaping the YouTube landscape. By keeping tabs on what others are doing, you stay in the loop with how online videos are being utilized. It's like attending a virtual industry conference without leaving your chair. You not only learn from others but also get a pulse on what matters to viewers.

In essence, leaving comments on YouTube videos is a multifaceted strategy that goes beyond mere engagement. It's about establishing yourself as a knowledgeable figure, connecting with a broader audience, boosting your views, and staying in tune with the pulse of the YouTube community. So, the next time you watch a video that sparks a thought or resonates with you, don't hesitate to drop a comment. Your words might just be the spark that ignites a meaningful connection, propelling you further into the vibrant world of online content creation.

The beauty of this whole shebang is that it's a two-way street. While you're building a community, your viewers are becoming your biggest advocates. They're not just passively watching; they're invested. They're sharing your videos, bringing in their friends, and creating a ripple effect that expands your reach faster than you can say "subscribe."

So, if you're serious about YouTube, it's time to put on your virtual party hat and start mingling in the comments section. Turn your channel into more than just a content hub—turn it into a thriving, buzzing community. Because when you talk to your viewers, you're not just making videos; you're building a tribe. And let's face it, who doesn't want a squad of loyal fans cheering them on every step of the way?

Challenge time: Well, by now you have your videos uploaded. I guess you have got some comments there. Get a specific time, during the day and reply to all those comments. Make sure that you at least create one long conversation from one of the comments as if you are talking to someone you have known for a while.

Chapter 8:

Making Money

At the moment, you may be starting this channel for fun, but everyone's long-term goal (always) is making money off it. Truth is, people have become millionaires from uploading videos, and you may wish to be one of them at some point.

The audience on YouTube is very big, and new viewers are always signing in every day and consuming countless hours of content every week. Not for nothing, in 2023, YouTube is expected to earn an astounding $30.4 billion in ad income.

The problem is making money from content can be challenging. Fortunately, there are several options available to you, depending on your content, audience, and marketing approach. But you shouldn't forego authenticity or entertainment value in favor of financial gain. This chapter covers the different ways you can make money.

Join the YouTube Partner Program

Here, there are no surprises! you can make money by having ads appear on your videos through the YouTube Partner Program.

Let's take a brief look at YouTube's Partner requirements. Assuming you comply with the monetization guidelines of the platform, you require:

- more than 4,000 genuine public watch hours in the last 12 months or 10 million legitimate public short views in the last 90 days

- more than 1,000 subscribers

- a linked and operational Google AdSense account

There are too many factors involved to provide a precise estimate of how much money you can generate from advertisements. Among these variables are:

- the demographics of your viewers, including age and location

- your kind of content

- whether your video has appropriate advertisers

Although "$1 per 1,000 views" was the standard in the past, things have changed. The Partner Program and ad regulations have changed in tandem with the YouTube algorithm. For instance, there are clear guidelines on the platform regarding advertising on YouTube Kids. Videos meant for children are excluded from a number of prominent ad categories and targeting options.

In any case, all you're looking at is a numbers game. Before you start making any significant money, each video must receive hundreds or even millions of views.

Unsure whether to run ads on your channel? Completely perceptible. Once more, video monetization shouldn't impede the expansion of your channel.

Your videos become almost unwatchable if they are overflowing with unskippable ads. However, a few advertisements here and there are completely acceptable.

Earn Support From Subscribers With a Channel Membership

Memberships for YouTube channels are made especially to help content creators, like you who want to monetize their work.

Consider memberships like Twitch or Patreon subscriptions. These subscribers pay a monthly charge. There are different membership tiers with different charges. In exchange for their money, they receive specific benefits, which might include conversation badges, premium material, and more. Depending on your membership tier, these advantages change.

You can upload video to YouTube exclusively instead of using a secondary channel. Memberships are a great idea if you publish content every day or if you stream live frequently. As of right now, channel membership eligibility is very similar to that of the Partner Program.

Put Promotional Links in Your Video Descriptions

Without displaying adverts, promo links are another way you can make money off of YouTube.

YouTube allows you a character count of 5,000, which is an important goldmine for your video descriptions. When you add these promo links in the description section, they will be exposed to your interested subscribers who may click on them. This may get you more clients. These links can be for:

- a free course or downloadable resource

- your website

- your merchandise or ecommerce shop

Feature Sponsors in Your Videos

Sponsored YouTube videos involve the explicit promotion of a brand within the video itself. Typically positioned at the video's outset and conclusion, these integrated ads are inseparable from the content, which makes them unskippable.

Such collaborations prove mutually beneficial for creators and advertisers, establishing a synergy that resonates positively with the audience.

Upload Product-Focused Promotional Videos

You make a branded video to specifically advertise a good or service. These videos can be divided into the following categories:

- You receive compensation from a brand in return for creating content or a review.

- The brand furnishes you with specific talking points and instructions.

- You produce a video to showcase and promote the brand while also generating affiliate revenue.

Leverage Affiliate Marketing

Affiliate marketing revolves around utilizing your influence to boost sales for external brands. As a content creator, you have the opportunity to collaborate with brands, endorsing their products or services within your content.

The concept is straightforward: you feature and discuss products in your videos, offering viewers a direct pathway to explore them. Each time a viewer clicks on your provided link and completes a purchase, you receive a commission. This arrangement benefits both parties, as brands gain increased visibility and sales, while you earn a share of the profits.

This approach is particularly prevalent among review channels and creators producing instructional content.

The crucial point is that the video doesn't exclusively focus on the products. Some creators mention their affiliate links in their content, while others choose not to. The decision is up to you!

Affiliate links are entirely permissible and comply with YouTube's Terms of Service. However, it's essential to be aware of the platform's explicit policy regarding external links. Before including links in your videos, take the time to familiarize yourself with YouTube's guidelines.

Take Advantage of Crowdfunding

Utilizing crowdfunding gives you an opportunity to build a bigger community while also getting funds for your content creation endeavors. It involves your fans collectively contributing to support your upcoming significant project.

Platforms such as Patreon provide a space for your supporters to make monthly contributions, gaining access to exclusive content and perks like behind-the-scenes footage, shoutouts, or early previews of upcoming videos.

Take, for instance, the cooking channel Made with Lau, which features three membership tiers on Patreon. They consistently promote their Patreon link in the descriptions of all their videos.

All you have to do is be sure to share the relevant link with your viewers and consistently deliver on the promises made.

Enable YouTube Super Chat & Super Stickers

Did you know that you can directly interact with your audience and receive money? It's possible through features like Super Chat & Stickers.

During a live stream, viewers have the option to pay for their messages to stand out in the chat. Also, they can send Super Stickers—animated images for which they pay, and these images then float up in the live chat.

For those who regularly host live sessions, leveraging Super Chats and Stickers proves to be an excellent method for enhancing engagement on YouTube, earning additional revenue, and fostering a positive connection with your audience. To enable Super Chat, go to your monetization settings.

It's essential to express gratitude and acknowledgment to viewers who support your channel by paying for enhanced interaction.

License Your Content to External Media Companies

Should your video go viral or feature something distinctive or newsworthy, other platforms or media sources may express interest in it. Licensing provides them the opportunity to utilize your content, albeit for a fee. This approach enables you to derive income from content you've already produced while extending its reach beyond your channel. Whether by proactively contacting media agencies or waiting for them to reach out to you, or by listing your content on platforms like Junkin Media, where TV channels and news sites can discover and acquire it, licensing offers a means to capitalize on your content's value.

Chapter 9:

The Power of Collaboration

As stated in the previous chapter, if you want to make a lot of money off YouTube, a big audience is key. So, one strategic move is reaching out to companies and collaborating with fellow YouTubers. This leads to growth and enhances the reach of your YouTube channel. In the dynamic nature of online content creation, forming partnerships can open doors to new audiences, provide valuable resources, and contribute to the overall development of your channel. This collaborative approach is multifaceted, as it involves engagement with both businesses and other content creators to create a synergistic effect that propels your channel forward.

One way you can expand your reach is through collaborations with companies. Companies are increasingly recognizing the value of influencer marketing, and YouTube is a prime platform for this strategy. Brands seek to leverage your established audiences to promote their products or services authentically. As a YouTuber, identifying brands that align with your content and resonate with your audience is crucial. This ensures that any partnership is seamless and enhances rather than detracts from your channel's authenticity.

Initiating contact with companies involves a strategic approach. You have to craft a compelling pitch that outlines the mutual benefits of collaboration. You must highlight your audience demographics, engagement metrics, and the unique value your channel brings. In your pitch, emphasize how this partnership can provide the company with exposure to a targeted audience and showcase your ability to integrate their products or services seamlessly into your content. Be clear about your expectations and deliverables while remaining open to negotiation.

Moreover, actively engaging with companies often goes beyond one-off collaborations. Building lasting relationships can lead to ongoing partnerships, sponsored content opportunities, and even product collaborations. These relationships can provide a consistent source of revenue and diversified content for your channel. Be transparent about your values and ensure that the companies you associate with align with your brand identity.

On the other hand, collaborating with fellow YouTubers is a dynamic strategy that can exponentially increase your channel's visibility. This type of partnership can take various forms, from co-creating content to cross-promoting each other's channels. The key is to find collaborators whose content complements yours without being in direct competition.

One effective collaboration method is creating joint videos. This could involve featuring another YouTuber on your channel, or vice versa. The shared audience between collaborators introduces each channel to a new set of potential subscribers. Additionally, the collaborative nature of these videos often leads to increased engagement, as viewers appreciate the novelty and chemistry between creators. An example of this is the collaboration of Niko Omilana and Jidion; they released a series of videos with a general title "The Biggest Menace." If you wanted to follow up and enjoy the whole series, you had to watch from both of their personal channels. This increased the views and engagement on both channels.

Cross-promotion is another powerful strategy when partnering with fellow YouTubers. This involves promoting each other's content on your respective channels or social media platforms. This mutual support can significantly expand your reach, especially if your collaborator has a larger or different audience demographic. Engaging with your collaborator's audience through comments and interactions can further solidify the connection and encourage cross-channel subscriptions.

Beyond the immediate benefits of increased visibility and subscriber growth, collaborations can also enhance your content quality. Exposure to different creative processes, styles, and perspectives can spark innovation and bring fresh ideas to your channel. Collaborating with others also provides an opportunity to tap into the collective knowledge and experience of the YouTube community.

Furthermore, collaborations can open doors to participation in broader initiatives, such as joint events, challenges, or community projects. These endeavors not only contribute to the growth of individual channels but also foster a sense of community within the broader YouTube ecosystem. Being an active participant in collaborative projects positions your channel as part of a larger network, which will potentially attracting new viewers interested in the collaborative community you contribute to.

To identify potential collaborators, explore YouTube within your niche or related genres. Look for creators with a similar subscriber count or slightly higher than yours, ensuring a balanced partnership. Reach out through social media or email, expressing your interest in collaboration and outlining the potential benefits for both parties. Clearly define the collaboration terms, such as video format, promotion strategy, and expected outcomes. This chapter covers the diverse ways through which you can connect with potential collaborators.

Direct Outreach

Engaging with a specific YouTuber for collaboration can be initiated through direct communication. You can do this through various channels such as the YouTuber's official website, their social media profiles, or, most notably, through their YouTube channel. When you establish contact in this manner, you may have an opportunity to build a relationship with them and even explore potential collaborative ventures.

Community Participation

Making sure that you become an active member of online communities that are dedicated to YouTube or specific niches is an effective strategy for connecting with like-minded creators. Platforms such as Facebook groups, subreddits, or Discord channels offer spaces where YouTubers can interact, share experiences, and identify potential collaboration opportunities.

Attendance at YouTube Events

Actively participating in YouTube-related events, including conventions, meetups, or creator summits, is a valuable networking opportunity. These events provide you a physical space to connect with fellow YouTubers, which leads to discussions on potential collaborations and expanding one's network within the YouTube community.

Collaboration Within Your Niche

Make sure that you identify and reach out to fellow YouTubers within your niche who produce content like yours. This is a strategic approach to collaboration. By establishing connections with creators whose content aligns with yours, you create opportunities for mutually beneficial collaborations that resonate with both audiences. And it is easier to get that collaboration.

Utilization of YouTube's Collaboration Feature

YouTube offers a dedicated collaboration feature that streamlines the process of working on joint video projects. This tool facilitates seamless cooperation between YouTubers, allowing you to create content together effortlessly. Leveraging this feature can enhance efficiency and enables the production of videos that cater to the interests of both collaborators' audiences.

Leverage Existing Networks

If you have already built relationships with other YouTubers, you should understand that leveraging existing networks can be a powerful method to secure collaboration opportunities. Building upon these already-established connections can enable you to tap into a network of potential collaborators and enrich their content through diverse partnerships.

Maintain Professionalism and Respect

When initiating contact with your potential collaborators, ensuring to maintain a professional and respectful tone is paramount. These may be your contemporaries, but you should understand that they don't know you that well. So, establish a respectful environment to build a good relationship with them. You should also clearly and carefully articulate collaborating your goals and expectations, as it helps establish a foundation for a successful partnership.

Prioritize Clarity in Agreements

You should also make sure that you establish clear agreements and an understanding of each other's expectations before embarking on a collaboration. This clarity ensures that both parties are on the same page regarding the scope and objectives of the collaboration.

In the pursuit of collaboration, you can extend an invitation to potential collaborators by encouraging them to follow your channel or visit your website. This is an open invitation, creating an accessible gateway for the interested parties to explore further collaboration opportunities. By creating an atmosphere of openness and approachability, you can attract like-minded individuals and nurture collaborative efforts that propel the growth of your YouTube channel.

In conclusion, reaching out to companies and collaborating with other YouTubers are integral strategies for growing your channel's reach. The dynamic landscape of online content creation demands a proactive approach to forming partnerships that align with your brand and goals. Whether engaging with companies for sponsored content or joining forces with fellow creators, the key is to build authentic connections that benefit all parties involved. Through strategic partnerships, you not only expand your audience but also enrich your content and contribute to the vibrant ecosystem of YouTube creators.

Homework: You now have your niche, and you did your research (as required in the previous chapters). Write down a list of the other Youtubers to would love to collaborate with:

_____

_____

_____

_____

_____

_____

_____

Chapter 10:

Your Influence Matters

Over the past decade, YouTube has evolved into a global platform that extends beyond mere entertainment, serving as a powerful tool for individuals to establish a substantial online presence.

So, you wanna be a YouTube influencer, huh? Well, it's not just about hitting a thousand subscribers—that's the golden ticket, apparently. You've got to carve out your own niche, be the guru of something, anything! DIY guru, gaming geek, makeup maestro—you name it.

Being an influencer is not all sunshine and rainbows. Behind those funny faces of influencers on camera, there's sweat, tears, and more editing than you can imagine. You need the tenacity of a bulldog and dedication that rivals a fitness freak on leg day. People are checking not just your sub count but also if you're the real deal. Are you trustworthy? Knowledgeable? Can they count on you for real info, not just a pretty face?

So, yeah, being a YouTube influencer seems like a blast, but it's a wild ride with its fair share of ups and downs. By the way, cheers to you for making it this far! This chapter will now cover the benefits of being an influencer.

Building a Personal Brand

One of the cardinal benefits of your YouTube influence is the ability to create and strengthen a personal brand. As a content creator, your unique voice, style, and perspective can resonate with a diverse audience. Successful YouTubers often become synonymous with their brand, which leads to a connection with viewers who appreciate their authenticity and content.

By consistently producing high-quality, engaging content, content creators can establish a recognizable brand that extends beyond the digital world. This, in turn, opens doors to opportunities such as brand collaborations, sponsorships, and merchandise sales. Building a personal brand through YouTube influence can lead to financial gains and long-term sustainability in the ever-evolving digital landscape.

Monetization and Financial Opportunities

YouTube's Partner Program empowers content creators to monetize their videos through advertising revenue, offering a substantial income source for influential YouTubers. The program's financial potential is directly correlated to a channel's subscriber count and views, making it imperative for creators to attract a large audience. Beyond ad revenue, savvy YouTubers can diversify their earnings through sponsored content, affiliate marketing, and crowdfunding (as discussed in the previous chapter).

Collaborating with companies for product or service promotion provides additional financial opportunities, which transforms your platform into a lucrative business. Successful negotiation and strategic partnerships play a crucial role in securing rewarding deals, which allows you to leverage your influence for sustainable income. As the program evolves, you are encouraged to explore and implement various revenue streams, which ensures the longevity and financial success of your YouTube ventures. The dynamic aspect of online content creation provides ample room for innovation and strategic monetization, which makes the YouTube Partner Program a vital tool for those aspiring to turn their passion into a profitable and sustainable career.

Career Opportunities and Entrepreneurship

Beyond monetary gains, a YouTube influence is also a gateway to diverse career opportunities. Many influencers seamlessly transition from content creation to roles like public speaking, consulting, and entrepreneurship. Establishing a personal brand on YouTube showcases a unique skill set that includes content creation, marketing prowess, and adept audience engagement. These skills become invaluable to businesses in search of digital expertise.

This influence also opens avenues for entrepreneurship, providing opportunities to launch personal products or services. Leveraging your influence, you can effortlessly introduce and promote these offerings to your audience, fostering a direct and often loyal customer base. This entrepreneurial journey not only diversifies income streams but also positions you as a creator with significant impact. The ability to navigate the dynamic landscape of online influence allows for a versatile career, emphasizing adaptability and innovation. In essence, a YouTube presence extends beyond entertainment, evolving into a multifaceted career that combines creativity, business acumen, and the potential to leave a lasting mark.

Educational and Inspirational Impact

YouTube influence is not solely about financial gains or career opportunities; it also provides a platform to educate and inspire. You can utilize your channel to share valuable knowledge, personal experiences, and expertise, which leaves a big impact on viewers. This educational outreach goes beyond traditional boundaries, influencing perspectives, sparking new interests, and even shaping career choices.

Beyond disseminating information, you can also often become a role model, motivating your audience to pursue passions and overcome challenges. The personal connection forged through online content allow you to create a positive impact, which leads to a sense of community and empowerment among your diverse viewership.

In this way, YouTube becomes a dynamic medium for not only entertainment but also for the dissemination of knowledge, the cultivation of inspiration, and the promotion of a supportive community, which makes it a significant force in shaping your life beyond the aspects of finance and career.

Social Change and Advocacy

With great influence comes the responsibility to contribute positively to society. When you recognize this, you will be able leverage your platform to advocate for social causes and highlight important issues. From addressing environmental concerns to promoting inclusivity and advocating for mental health awareness, you can be in position use your reach to amplify crucial messages with authority.

This influence is a powerful tool for social change, which allow you to mobilize your audience toward collective action. This advocacy not only raises awareness but also contributes to meaningful change, showcasing the potential of YouTube as a force for good in the world. By harnessing your big audience, you become an agent of positive transformation, fostering a sense of community engagement and responsibility.

In an era where digital platforms play a vital role in shaping public opinion, you wield significant impact. Your commitment to advocating for social issues demonstrates the broader potential of online platforms to serve as catalysts for positive change, proving that with influence comes the ability to shape a better, more socially conscious world.

While YouTube influence offers numerous opportunities, it comes with its share of challenges and responsibilities. You have to go through a lot of issues such as maintaining authenticity, managing your mental health, and addressing potential controversies. The responsibility to influence responsibly is paramount, considering the impact influencers can have on their audience.

Maintaining Authenticity

Sustaining authenticity poses a significant challenge for YouTube influencers. As you navigate this competitive journey, the pressure to conform or cater to trends may compromise the genuine connection with your audience. Striking a balance between staying true to your identity and adapting to evolving content demands is crucial. The authenticity challenge demands constant self-reflection and a commitment to originality, which ensures that you remain a trusted voice in your niche.

Managing Mental Health

This relentless nature of the digital world can take a toll on your mental health. The constant scrutiny, comments, and pressure to perform consistently can lead to burnout and emotional exhaustion. Balancing personal well-being with the demands of content creation becomes essential.

So, to mitigate this challenge, you should establish healthy boundaries, seeking support and periodically disconnecting from the online world.

Addressing Potential Controversies

You also find yourself in the spotlight, which makes you susceptible to controversies that can impact your reputation and influence. Navigating these situations requires a delicate touch, with you needing to address issues transparently, take responsibility for your actions, and learn from mistakes. Successfully managing potential controversies demands effective communication skills and a strategic approach to maintain trust and credibility within your audience.

Responsibility to Influence Responsibly

This influence comes with a significant responsibility. Recognizing the potential impact on your audience, you must exercise care in the content you produce. This involves considering the ethical implications of your influence, avoiding harmful behaviors, and promoting positive values. Balancing the desire for engagement with the need to influence responsibly requires a keen awareness of the potential consequences of your reach and impact on viewers.

Additionally, the evolving landscape of digital platforms requires constant adaptation and staying abreast of industry trends. You must remain agile, embracing new technologies and strategies to stay relevant and continue growing your influence over time.

In conclusion, YouTube influence will present a lot of opportunities to you, in case you are willing to invest time, effort, and creativity into your channel. From building a personal brand and monetizing content to pursuing entrepreneurial ventures and advocating for social change, the potential impact of YouTube influence is very big.

But as you celebrate your YouTube influence, it is crucial to approach this journey with a sense of responsibility and a commitment to authenticity. By leveraging influence wisely, you can not only achieve personal and financial success but also make a positive and lasting impact on their audience and society at large.

Chapter 11:

The Video Formula

With all that we have discussed in the previous chapters, this is a summary of how you can create engaging and impactful videos. It requires a thoughtful approach and a strategic formula. This step-by-step guide will help you plan, shoot, and edit videos with purpose and precision.

Step 1: Define Your Purpose and Audience

Before diving into the video creation process, clearly define the purpose of your video and identify your target audience. Ask yourself:

- What message do you want to convey?

- Who is your intended audience?

- What action do you want viewers to take after watching?

Understanding your purpose and audience will guide all subsequent decisions in the video creation process.

Step 2: Develop a Compelling Concept

Once you've established your purpose and audience, brainstorm and develop a compelling concept for your video. Consider the following elements:

- **Storyline:** Craft a narrative that resonates with your audience. Whether it's educational, entertaining, or emotional, a strong storyline captures attention.

- **Hook:** Create a captivating hook in the first few seconds to grab viewers' attention. This could be a question, intriguing statement, or visually striking scene.

- **Value proposition:** Clearly communicate the value viewers will gain from watching your video. What problem will you solve, or what information will you provide?

Step 3: Plan Your Content and Structure

Outline the content of your video, ensuring a logical and engaging flow. Consider these aspects:

- **Introduction:** Briefly introduce yourself or your brand. Clearly state the purpose of the video and what viewers can expect.

- **Main content:** Organize your main points logically. Use a mix of visuals, demonstrations, and explanations to convey information effectively.

- **Call to action (CTA):** Clearly define the desired action you want viewers to take after watching the video. It could be subscribing, sharing, visiting a website, or any other relevant action.

Step 4: Script Your Dialogue

Craft a script that aligns with your concept and content plan. While spontaneity is valuable, having a script ensures clarity and coherence. Consider the following tips:

- **Conversational tone:** Write the script in a conversational tone as it would help to connect with your audience. Avoid jargon or overly formal language unless it suits your brand or content.

- **Visual cues:** Note where specific visuals, demonstrations, or graphics will be incorporated. This helps maintain a seamless connection between your script and the visual elements.

- **Length:** Keep your script concise and focused. Attention spans are limited, so aim for a duration that effectively conveys your message without unnecessary filler.

Step 5: Gather Your Equipment

Make sure you have the required gear before you start shooting. This doesn't imply you have to have the best equipment; you can create excellent content with a smartphone that has a respectable camera. Gather the following:

- **Camera:** Use a camera that suits your needs. If you're just starting, a smartphone camera can be more than sufficient.

- **Microphone:** Clear audio is crucial. Invest in an external microphone or use the built-in microphone on your camera.

- **Tripod:** Stabilize your shots with a tripod. This is especially important for static shots or if you're recording yourself.

- **Lighting:** Natural light is ideal, but if that's not possible, invest in soft, diffused lighting to avoid harsh shadows.

Step 6: Plan Your Shots and Visuals

Visual appeal is key to keeping viewers engaged. Plan your shots and visuals in advance:

- **B-roll:** Capture additional footage, known as B-roll, to complement your main content. This could include close-ups, demonstrations, or relevant scenes that enhance storytelling.

- **Transitions:** Plan how you'll transition between different shots or scenes. Smooth transitions maintain flow and professionalism.

- **Graphics and text:** If your video requires graphics or text overlays, plan where these elements will appear and what information they'll convey.

Step 7: Record Your Video

It's time to start recording now that your gear is assembled, and the shots are planned. For a productive recording session, follow these tips:

- **Environment:** Choose a quiet, well-lit space. Minimize background noise and distractions.

- **Camera settings:** Ensure your camera settings are optimized for video recording. Pay attention to resolution, frame rate, and focus.

- **Test shots:** Take a few test shots to check lighting, framing, and audio quality before recording your main content.

- **Natural delivery:** Speak naturally and maintain eye contact with the camera. If you're demonstrating something, ensure it's visible and understandable.

Step 8: Edit Your Video

Editing is where your raw footage transforms into a polished, cohesive video. Consider the following steps:

- **Trimming:** Remove unnecessary footage and trim any awkward pauses or mistakes.

- **Transitions:** Add smooth transitions between clips to maintain flow.

- **Graphics and text:** Incorporate any planned graphics or text overlays.

- **Music:** If appropriate, add background music to enhance the mood of your video.

- **Color Correction:** Adjust colors and tones for a consistent and appealing look.

Step 9: Optimize for SEO and Accessibility

Before publishing, optimize your video for search engines and accessibility:

- **Title:** Create a compelling title that accurately represents your content and includes relevant keywords.

- **Description:** Write a detailed video description, incorporating keywords naturally. Provide additional information, links, and timestamps.

- **Tags:** Use relevant tags to improve discoverability.

- **Closed captions:** To reach a larger audience, add subtitles or closed captions to your video.

Step 10: Publish and Promote

Once your video is polished and optimized, it's time to share it with the world:

- **Engagement:** Interact with comments and actively engage with your audience. This fosters a sense of community and motivates viewers to come back for more.

- **Promotion:** Share your video on social media, in relevant groups, or through email newsletters to increase visibility.

Step 11: Analyze and Learn

After your video is live, analyze its performance:

- **Metrics:** Review metrics such as views, watch time, and engagement.

- **Audience insights:** Use analytics tools to understand your audience better. Where are they located? What age group do they belong to?

- **Feedback:** Pay attention to comments and feedback. Use constructive criticism to improve future videos.

Step 12: Iterate and Improve

Apply the insights gained from analytics and feedback to iterate and improve your future videos. Continual improvement is key to building a loyal audience and enhancing the effectiveness of your video content.

By following "The Video Formula," you'll be equipped to plan, shoot, and edit videos that captivate your audience, deliver value, and achieve your intended goals. Regardless of your level of experience, this thorough guide offers a road map for producing engaging and compelling videos.

YouTube Support

In case you have any questions, or you need help on the platform, you can visit the following links:

Check to see whether your content is appropriate for kids:

https://support.google.com/youtube/answer/9528076

Copyright:

https://www.youtube.com/intl/ALL_uk/howyoutubeworks/policies/copyright/

YouTube community guidelines:

https://www.youtube.com/howyoutubeworks/policies/community-guidelines/#community-guidelines

Account security and tips for staying safe online:

https://support.google.com/youtube/answer/2802848?hl=en&ref_topic=9386941

YouTube Creator academy:

https://creatoracademy.youtube.com/page/course/bootcamp-foundations?

Minimum age requirements:

https://support.google.com/accounts/answer/1350409

Getting a customer URL:

https://support.google.com/youtube/answer/2657968?

Staying safe on YouTube:

https://support.google.com/youtube/answer/9563682?

Staying safe as a teen:

https://support.google.com/youtube/answer/2802244?

Best practices for content with children:

https://support.google.com/youtube/answer/9229229?

YouTube families & parent resources:

https://support.google.com/youtube/answer/2802272?

Child safety on YouTube:

https://support.google.com/youtube/answer/2801999?

Parent resources:

https://support.google.com/youtube/answer/2802272?

Parental controls and settings:

https://support.google.com/youtubekids/answer/6172308?

Conclusion

As you conclude the exhilarating journey of pursuing YouTube success, you'll need to recognize the evolving responsibility that comes with growing from a teenager into adulthood. Your videos carry influence, and as your audience broadens, so does your impact. There's a responsibility to avoid promoting wasteful ideas, reckless behavior, and other potentially harmful content. Remember, kids will be watching, and they might mimic your speech and actions in the real world. Consider the potential impact of your content on impressionable minds and think about the values and messages you want to convey.

This adventure is not solely about views and likes; it's about connecting with people who resonate with your unique style. If you're a teen with dreams of YouTube stardom, keep those creative juices flowing and embrace the quirks that make you, well, you. As you navigate this space, keep in mind the evolving nature of your audience and the impact your content can have. Be authentic, responsible, and mindful of the influence you wield, ensuring your journey contributes positively to the YouTube community.

Success on YouTube is like planting a garden—it takes time, care, and a bit of trial and error. Sure, you might hit a few bumps along the way, but that's all part of the adventure. Don't stress about the numbers too much; focus on creating content that you genuinely love. Your passion will shine through and attract the right crowd—your virtual squad who's here for the real you.

Collaborate, experiment, and don't be afraid to switch things up. After all, trends come and go faster than you can say "subscribe." Stay true to what makes you happy, and chances are, you'll make your audience happy, too. Remember, even the big-shot YouTubers started small, probably with some cringe-worthy videos (we all have those hidden in the archives).

And hey, don't forget to take breaks. YouTube success is exciting, but burnout is not a good look on anyone. Balance is the key—balance between your online life and the real world, between creating content and enjoying the fruits of your labor.

Top tip: Schedule regular breaks to recharge, both mentally and physically. Your creativity will thank you, and your audience will appreciate the consistently fresh energy you bring to your content.

Practical: I will create content for ___ *days, and I will take* ___ days off each week to enjoy life as it unfolds naturally (plus special events!).

In the world of YouTube, there's always room for new voices and fresh perspectives. So, grab that camera, hit record, and enjoy the rollercoaster of YouTube success—at the end of the day, it's not just about the destination; it's about the hilarious, challenging, and downright awesome journey you're on. Happy YouTubing!

References

Barnhart, B. (2022, August 23). *How to make money on YouTube (and what creators should expect).* Sprout Social. https://sproutsocial.com/insights/how-to-make-money-on-youtube/

Bedrina, O. (2019). *12 Simple Tips for Making Your Videos Look More Professional.* Wave.video Blog. https://wave.video/blog/12-simple-tips-for-making-your-videos-look-more-professional/

Bump, P. (2021, May 5). *7 YouTube Features That Will Help You Get More Views.* Blog.hubspot.com. https://blog.hubspot.com/blog/tabid/6307/bid/5886/5-youtube-features-to-get-more-video-views.aspx

Commenting on Videos Can Help Your Video Marketing. (n.d.). Gearshift Studios. Retrieved December 3, 2023, from https://www.gearshift.tv/library/comment-on-youtube-videos-to-increase-views---subscribers.cfm#:~:text=Commenting%20on%20Videos%20Can%20Help%20Your%20Video%20Marketing&text=One%20of%20the%20best%20ways

Monthly content plan: 7 steps to get started. (2022, November 25). Locowise Blog. https://locowise.com/blog/monthly-content-plan-7-steps-to-get-started

V, S. (2021, January 29). *Worried about Content Creation?* Medium. https://medium.datadriveninvestor.com/worried-about-content-creation-6a00fc8799c8

YouTube SEO Optimization Tips: Rank For Video Content In 2023. (n.d.). BrightEdge. Retrieved December 3, 2023, from https://www.brightedge.com/glossary/youtube-seo-and-search-trends#:~:text=YouTube%20optimization%20focuses%20on%20the